CCSS Genre Fantasy

Essential Question
What buildings do you know?
What are they made of?

by Vita Jiménez
illustrated by Neecy Twinem

Chapter 1

Tommy and Steve

Tommy lives in the city. He has lived there his whole life. He likes the brick buildings and the sidewalks full of people.

Steve lives in the country. He has lived there his whole life. He is Tommy's cousin. Steve likes the homes made of wood. He likes the dirt streets and farmland.

Steve has not seen Tommy for many years. One day, he decides to visit him. Steve packs three sandwiches for the trip. Then he gets on a bus.

Chapter 2

A Visit to the City

Tommy is happy to see Steve. He takes Steve around the big city. They pass apartment buildings and see many people.

"The buildings are tall and strong," says Tommy.

"But it is hard to see the sky," says Steve.

"You could get used to that," says Tommy.

Later, Steve eats pizza for the first time. After a while, Steve misses the country. Now Tommy will go see where Steve lives. They buy sandwiches for the long trip.

Chapter 3

A Visit to the Country

When they arrive, Steve shows Tommy his farmhouse.

"This wood house keeps you warm?" asks Tommy.

"Yes, it does," says Steve.

They walk around and look at the
sky. Then they pick some corn.
Now Tommy's shiny shoes are dirty.

"I like to live in the city better,"
he says.

Chapter 4

Home Sweet Home

The next day, Tommy goes back home. He feels safe and warm in his brick building. He eats sweet corn and thinks of Steve. He will visit Steve again soon.

Steve is safe and warm in his wooden farmhouse. He makes a pizza and thinks of Tommy. One day he will visit Tommy again.

Respond to Reading

Retell

Use your own words to retell events in *City Armadillo, Country Armadillo.*

Character	Setting	Events

Text Evidence

1. Who are the characters in the story? What are they like? Character, Setting, Events

2. Where does Tommy live? Where does Steve live? Character, Setting, Events

3. How do you know this story is a fantasy? Genre

Compare Texts

What's different about life in the city and life in the country?

City or Country?

Let's look at the city.

There are tall buildings.

The roads are paved.

There are lots of cars and buses.

Look at all the people.

Let's look at the country.

There are barns.

Some roads are dirt.

There are lots of cornfields.

Look at the horses.

Make Connections

Look at both selections. What did you learn about the city and the country?

Text to Text

Focus on  Genre

Fantasy Fantasy is a story that has invented characters, settings, or events that could not be real.

What to Look for In *City Armadillo, Country Armadillo*, the armadillos talk, wear clothes, and buy sandwiches and pizza. Real armadillos don't do these things.

Your Turn

Pretend you're a talking animal that lives in the forest. You have a cousin that lives by the sea. Write two or three sentences to tell how your homes are alike or different.